Angel Number Handbook
By J. Brownbridge.

This book is dedicated to Zuzu and Manfred.
My Loves.

Angel numbers are a form of spiritual guidance believed to be sent from the divine realm. They are said to be messages from our guardian angels, or other divine beings, that can help us understand our life's purpose and direction. Angel numbers are also seen as a way to connect with the divine and receive direct guidance and understanding.

Angel numbers are usually seen as repeating sequences of numbers, such as 1111 or 333. Each number carries its own unique meaning and significance, so it is important to take the time to understand what each number means for you personally. For example, angel number 1111 is often associated with new beginnings, fresh starts, and manifesting your desires into reality. Alternatively, angel number 333 may be seen as a sign of encouragement from the angels that you are on the right path in life and should continue to follow your heart's true desires.

When we receive angel numbers in our lives, it is important to take the time to meditate on them and really explore their meanings for us. It may also be helpful to keep a journal of any angel numbers you come across during your day-to-day life so that you can look back at them later for further exploration and understanding.

Ultimately, angel numbers can provide incredible insight into our lives if we take the time to pay attention and interpret their meaning for us personally. They can help guide us towards our true destiny and lead us towards a more meaningful life full of love and light.

## 111

Angel number 111 is a powerful sign from the divine realm that encourages us to stay positive and focus on our goals. It is a reminder that we are being supported by the Universe and that our thoughts, words, and actions are creating our reality.

The number 111 is a combination of the numbers 1 and 11, which both have powerful meanings. The number 1 symbolizes new beginnings, fresh starts, and taking initiative. It encourages us to take action and trust in ourselves. The number 11 is associated with spiritual awakening, intuition, and enlightenment. It reminds us to stay connected to our higher selves and trust in the divine guidance we receive.

When angel number 111 appears in your life it is a sign that you are on the right path towards achieving your goals. It is an indication that you should stay focused on your intentions and trust in the Universe's support.

This angelic message also encourages you to be open to new opportunities as they arise, as they may be part of your divine plan for success. Angel number 111 can also be seen as a reminder to stay positive no matter what challenges come your way.

This angelic message encourages us to remain optimistic even when things seem difficult or uncertain. By staying positive we can attract more positive energy into our lives which will help us manifest our desires more quickly and easily.

In conclusion, angel number 111 is a powerful sign from the divine realm that encourages us to stay focused on our goals while remaining open to new opportunities as they arise. It reminds us to stay positive no matter what challenges come our way so that we can manifest our desires more quickly and easily with the help of the Universe's support.

## 222

Angel number 222 is a powerful sign from the divine realm that encourages you to stay positive and trust that everything will work out in your favour. It is a reminder to stay focused on your goals and trust that the Universe is supporting you in manifesting your desires.

The number 222 is composed of two 2s, which represent balance, harmony, duality, and cooperation. It symbolizes the need to find balance between your spiritual and material life. This number also encourages you to be open to new opportunities and take risks in order to achieve success.

The angel number 222 also signifies faith and trust in the Universe. It reminds you that whatever happens in life, it is all part of a greater plan for your highest good. This number encourages you to have faith that everything will work out for the best even if it doesn't seem like it at first.

The angel number 222 also symbolizes abundance and prosperity. It reminds you that abundance comes from within and that by focusing on positive thoughts and feelings, you can attract more abundance into your life. This number encourages you to be grateful for what you have already achieved and open yourself up to receive more blessings from the Universe.

In conclusion, angel number 222 is a powerful sign from the divine realm that encourages us to stay positive, trust in the Universe, find balance between our spiritual and material lives, take risks, have faith, be grateful for what we have already achieved, and open ourselves up to receive more blessings from the Universe.

## 333

The angel number 333 is a powerful sign from the angels that signifies growth and expansion. It is a message of encouragement to stay on your path and trust in the divine guidance that is available to you.

The number 3 symbolizes creativity, joy, enthusiasm, and spiritual growth.

When you see the angel number 333, it is a reminder to stay focused on your goals and dreams. It encourages you to take action and have faith in yourself and your journey. The angels are reminding you that you are fully supported by them as you strive towards your goals. They are with you every step of the way, providing guidance, protection, and love.
The angel number 333 also symbolizes your connection with the divine realm. It reminds you that the Universe has your back at all times and will provide for all of your needs. You are encouraged to trust in yourself and in the support of spirit guides as they help guide you along your path.

The angel number 333 also serves as a reminder to be kinder to yourself. This is an important reminder because when we treat ourselves with love and compassion we are more likely to be open to receiving messages from our angels. We can also create more positive energy around us when we take care of ourselves physically, mentally, emotionally, and spiritually.

Finally, the angel number 333 signifies abundance in all areas of life; it encourages us to stay connected with our higher selves so that we can manifest our dreams into reality. Whenever this number appears in our lives it is a reminder that all things are possible when we align ourselves with our true purpose in life!

## 444

Angel number 444 is a powerful message from the divine realm that signifies that you are being watched over and protected by your guardian angels.

This number is a reminder to trust in yourself and your intuition, as it is a sign of divine guidance. It also encourages you to stay positive and to keep your faith strong.

When angel number 444 appears in your life, it can be interpreted as a message of encouragement and support from the angels. This number reminds us that our guardian angels are here for us, providing us with strength, protection, and guidance. It is a reminder to stay focused on our goals and aspirations, and to trust in the process of life.

This number also serves as a reminder that we are never alone; even in our darkest moments, our angels are there for us.

Angel number 444 can also be interpreted as an indicator of abundance and prosperity coming into our lives. The angels may be sending this message to remind us that they are working on our behalf to bring forth

good fortune and blessings into our lives. When we are open to this energy, we can create abundance in all areas of life – physical, emotional, mental, spiritual, and financial. In conclusion, angel number 444 is an uplifting sign of divine love and support from the universe. It is a reminder that we have guardian angels looking out for us at all times; they provide strength when we need it most and serve as messengers of hope when times seem dark or uncertain.
 This number encourages us to remain positive in all circumstances and trust in the power of prayer – as it will bring forth blessings into our lives if we remain open-minded and faithful.

## 555

Angel number 555 is a powerful sign from the Universe that signifies a major life change. It is a message of encouragement from your guardian angels, urging you to embrace the changes that are coming and to have faith in yourself and the Universe.

The number 5 is the most frequent number to appear in angel numbers, as it is associated with personal freedom, adventure, and curiosity. When this number appears three times consecutively, it carries an even more profound message.

555 encourages us to let go of our fears and embrace change with enthusiasm and optimism. It also symbolizes our willingness to take risks, explore new possibilities, and strive for growth and success. When we encounter angel number 555, it can be a sign that our current situation is no longer serving us or that there are better opportunities ahead if we are willing to make some changes. Whether this means changing jobs or relationships, moving to a new city, or simply taking up a new hobby or activity—555 encourages us to trust in ourselves and take action towards something new and exciting.

Angel number 555 also serves as a reminder of the power of positive thinking. The Universe will often give us what we focus on, so if we focus on fear or doubt we will only attract more of those energies into our lives. On the other hand, if we choose to focus on optimism and confidence in ourselves and our abilities—we will be rewarded with greater success and abundance in all areas of our lives.

In conclusion, angel number 555 is a powerful sign from the Universe reminding us that change can bring great rewards if we are willing to embrace it with an open heart and mind. By trusting in ourselves, having faith in the Universe's plan for us, and focusing on positive thoughts—we can manifest great abundance into our lives.

## 666

Angel number 666 isn't always bad, it also has a deep spiritual significance and is a sign from your guardian angels that you are being watched over and protected.

This number symbolizes balance and harmony, as well as the completion of a cycle or process. This number can also be seen as a warning to stay alert, as it can be an indication that something bad may be coming your way.

In addition to its spiritual meaning, angel number 666 can also represent material wealth and abundance. It is believed that if you see this number regularly, it could be a sign of financial success in the near future. It can also signify good luck in business or other ventures, so if you're looking for a new job or business opportunity then this could be an auspicious sign for you.

Finally, angel number 666 can represent transformation and growth. If you've been feeling stuck in life or like something needs to change then seeing this number might be an indication that something new is on its way. The universe may be sending you a message that it's time to make some changes in order to move forward in life and reach your goals.

In conclusion, angel number 666 carries many different meanings depending on how it appears in your life. Ultimately though, its primary interpretation is one of protection and guidance from your guardian angels; they are watching over you and helping guide you down the right path towards success and happiness.

777

Angel number 777 is a powerful symbol of spiritual guidance and enlightenment. The number 777 is associated with the spiritual realm and its energies, as well as with luck and success. It is believed that when this number appears in your life, it is a sign that angels are watching over you and are ready to help you manifest your desires.

The number 777 has many different meanings, but the most common interpretation is that it represents divine completion or the completion of something significant in your life. It can be a sign from the universe that you are on the right path, or it can be an indication of success and good fortune coming your way.

In addition to being a sign of divine completion, angel number 777 also symbolizes good luck. This could mean that you are about to experience a period of great luck or fortune in some area of your life. It could also be an indication that you will soon receive guidance from the angels on how to make the most out of any situation.

The meaning behind angel number 777 may vary depending on your individual circumstances and beliefs, but one thing is certain: when this number appears in your life, it's time to pay attention! If you have been feeling lost or confused about where to go next in life, this could be a sign from above that now is the time to take action and make positive changes in your life.

No matter what challenges or obstacles may come up along the way, angel number 777 can serve as a reminder that you're not alone on this journey — there's always help available when you ask for it! So, keep an open mind and heart and trust that everything will work out for the best.

## 888

The angel number 888 is a powerful symbol of abundance, prosperity, and success. This number represents the power of the spiritual realm and its connection to the material world. It is often seen as a sign that great blessings are on their way, or that something positive is happening in one's life.

The number 888 can be broken down into three parts: 8+8+8=24. The number 24 is associated with the energy of justice, balance, and harmony. It can be interpreted as a sign that things are being balanced out in one's life, or that justice will be served. This could mean that any negative energy or karma from past actions is being cleared away to make room for positive blessings.

The number 8 itself has a strong spiritual significance in many cultures and religions around the world. In Christianity, it symbolizes resurrection and new beginnings. In Chinese culture it is associated with wealth and good fortune. The eight-pointed star is also used as a symbol for abundance and good luck in many cultures around the world.

When you see the angel number 888 it can also be a reminder to stay focused on your goals and dreams. It can encourage you to take action towards achieving your desires by setting clear intentions and working hard to bring them into reality. The angel number 888 can also remind you to stay humble and grateful for all of life's blessings, no matter how small they may seem.

In conclusion, the angel number 888 carries a powerful message of abundance, prosperity, success, justice, balance, harmony, new beginnings, wealth, and good fortune. It encourages us to stay focused on our goals while staying humble and grateful for all our blessings in life.

## 999

Angel number 999 is a powerful message from the divine realm that symbolizes the completion of a spiritual journey or cycle. It is a sign of closure and finality, and it suggests that you should be prepared for the next chapter in your life. This number is often associated with spiritual awakening, enlightenment, and ascension.

The number nine has multiple meanings in numerology. It is seen as a number of completion because it represents the end of a cycle, just like the angel number 999. Nine is also associated with humanitarianism and compassion, suggesting that you should strive to be more compassionate towards yourself and others. It could also mean that you are on the verge of achieving something great if you remain focused on your goals and stay true to yourself.

The number nine can also represent spiritual growth and transformation, which means that angel number 999 could be urging you to take steps towards achieving your highest potential in life. This could range from taking up new hobbies or activities to developing new skills or exploring different facets of yourself. It could also mean reaching out for help when needed or seeking guidance from mentors or spiritual advisors when necessary.

Overall, angel number 999 is a powerful reminder to stay focused on your goals while remaining compassionate towards yourself and those around you. It suggests that you are close to completing a major cycle in your life and encourages you to take advantage of this opportunity to reach your highest potential by taking risks and exploring new possibilities.

## 1111

Angel number 1111 is a powerful and meaningful number that has been seen by many people around the world. It is a sign from the angels that something important is happening in your life and you should pay attention to the messages they are sending.

The number 1 symbolizes new beginnings, fresh starts, creativity, and progress. It is a reminder to stay positive and have faith in yourself and your abilities. Seeing this number could be a sign that you are about to embark on a new journey or take steps towards achieving your goals.

The combination of four 1s also suggests that the angels are sending you additional guidance or support. They want you to know that they are with you every step of the way and will help guide you when needed. This can be especially helpful if you're feeling stuck or overwhelmed with life's challenges.

The angel number 1111 also represents alignment with your true purpose in life. It can be interpreted as an invitation to explore what it is that truly inspires and motivates you, so that you can focus your energy on living a more fulfilling life.

Finally, seeing this number could be an indication that something big is coming your way soon. It could be an opportunity for growth or a chance to make some much-needed changes in your life. Whatever it may be, it's important to remember that whatever happens will be for the best in the long run.

In conclusion, angel number 1111 carries deep spiritual significance and should not be taken lightly. It's an encouraging reminder from the angels to stay positive, have faith in yourself, and follow your true purpose in life – no matter what comes your way!

2222

Angel number 2222 is a powerful sign from the divine realm. It is a message from your angels that you are on the right path, and they are supporting and guiding you every step of the way. This angel number also stands for balance, harmony, and peace in your life.

When you see this angel number, it is a sign that you should trust in yourself and your decisions. You are being encouraged to stay positive and have faith that everything will work out for your highest good. Your angels are giving you the strength to stay focused on your goals and trust that the Universe is providing all the support you need.

The number 2222 symbolizes duality, which means there is both light and dark in life. It reminds us to accept both positive and negative experiences as part of our journey. We must learn to be open to new opportunities while also learning from our mistakes. This angel number encourages us to embrace all aspects of life with an open heart and mind so we can grow spiritually.

The number 2222 also stands for patience, understanding, cooperation, and compromise when dealing with difficult situations or people in our lives. It encourages us to be tolerant of others' opinions even if they differ from ours, as well as being kinder to ourselves when things don't go our way.

Overall, angel number 2222 is an important reminder from the divine realm that we should stay true to ourselves while also having an open mind towards others' perspectives. By embracing duality with patience and understanding, we can create balance in our lives and manifest all our desires into reality!

3333

The angel number 3333 is a powerful and meaningful number. It is seen as a sign of encouragement from the angels, and it can bring about positive changes in your life.

The number 3333 is associated with creativity, growth, and optimism. It is believed to signify the divine presence of the angels in your life, as well as their guidance and protection. This number can also represent potential opportunities for you to explore or develop new skills or talents. The angels may be guiding you towards something that could bring you joy or success.

The number 3333 can also be a sign of completion or closure on something that has been bothering you for some time. It may mean that it's time to move on from a particular situation, issue, or relationship that no longer serves you. This angelic message encourages you to let go of any negative feelings and emotions so that you can make room for new beginnings in your life.

Additionally, angel number 3333 can be seen as an indication of spiritual growth and enlightenment. If this is the case, then it's a reminder to stay open-minded and remain curious about the world around us. The angels may be encouraging us to explore our spirituality further, learn more about our true selves, and open our hearts to love and compassion for others.

In conclusion, angel number 3333 is an incredibly powerful symbol of encouragement from the angels that can bring about positive changes in your life if you choose to accept it. Whether this means letting go of something old or embracing something new, this angelic message could be just what you need to take your life in a new direction!

## 4444

Angel number 4444 is an incredibly powerful sign from the divine realm. It is a message of support and guidance from your angels, letting you know that you are on the right path and that they are with you all the way. The number 4 has a special significance in numerology, as it resonates with the vibrations of practicality, hard work, stability, honesty, and integrity.

When angel number 4444 appears in your life it's a sign that it's time to focus on building solid foundations for yourself and for your future. Your angels want you to know that if you put in the hard work now, then you will reap the rewards further down the line. It's a reminder to stay focused on your goals and to take things one step at a time.

The number 4 also symbolizes strong foundations such as family and home life. This angel number is encouraging you to nurture these relationships and to create a safe and secure environment for yourself and those around you. It is also asking you to be more organized in all aspects of your life so that everything runs more smoothly.

Seeing angel number 4444 is like having an extra pair of hands helping you out along the way. Your angels are here to support and guide you so don't be afraid to ask for help when needed. They want nothing more than for you to succeed in everything that you do!

5555

The meaning of angel number 5555 is one of positivity and encouragement. This number is a sign from the angels that they are with you, and they want to help you make the most out of your life. It's a reminder that the universe is constantly working in your favour, and that you should take advantage of any opportunities that come your way.

Angel number 5555 is also a sign of progress and growth. It encourages you to keep striving towards your goals, no matter how difficult it may be. The angels want you to stay focused on what's important, and not let any negative thoughts or feelings hold you back from achieving success. They are sending you positive energy to help you stay motivated and on track. The message behind angel number 5555 is one of abundance and prosperity. This number can signify a new beginning for you, as well as an opportunity for financial gain or increased wealth. It's a reminder that the universe will provide if we have faith in ourselves and our abilities. The angels want us to be confident in our decisions, so we can make the most out of our lives. In conclusion, angel number 5555 is a sign from the angels that they are with us every step of the way, encouraging us to stay positive and motivated on our journey towards success. They are reminding us to keep striving for our goals, no matter what obstacles may come our way. If we have faith in ourselves and trust in the universe's guidance, we can make the most out of our lives!

6666

Angel number 6666 is a powerful sign of manifesting abundance, success, and progress in all areas of life. It is a call from the angels to stay focused on your true purpose and divine mission in life. This number indicates that you are about to experience a major shift in your life that will bring you closer to achieving your goals.

The number 6666 is composed of two master numbers – 6 and 6. The number 6 stands for balance, harmony, stability, and responsibility. It also symbolizes family and home life. The second 6 represents material abundance, financial security, and success. Together these two numbers suggest that you are being asked to take responsibility for your life and focus on manifesting abundance in all aspects of it.

When angel number 6666 appears in your life it is an indication that you are on the right path to achieving your goals. You have been working hard towards manifesting positive outcomes and the angels are sending their support to help you along the way. Your faith in yourself and the Universe will result in great rewards both spiritually and materially.

This angelic number also encourages you to be generous with others by sharing what you have with those around you. This could be anything from time or money to advice or emotional support – whatever it may be, it will come back to you tenfold as a reward for being kind-hearted and generous with those around you.

In conclusion, angel number 6666 is a powerful sign from the angels that indicates progress towards success in all areas of life – both material wealth as well as spiritual growth. It encourages us to stay focused on our true purpose while remaining generous with others so that we may receive abundant blessings from the Universe in return.

7777

Angel number 7777 is an angelic sign from the spiritual realm that carries a powerful message of abundance and success. It is a reminder that the universe is always providing us with support, guidance, and protection. It is a sign of abundance, good luck, and inner peace.

The number 7 has been associated with spiritual enlightenment, success, and divine power since ancient times. In numerology, it symbolizes completion, knowledge, and wisdom. The double sevens in this angel number signify a higher level of spiritual awareness and an increased connection to the divine realm.

When you see this number in your life it can be a sign from the angels that you are on the right path in life and that you should continue to stay focused on your goals. The angels are sending you their love and encouragement to help you manifest your dreams into reality. They want you to trust that your hard work will pay off soon and that all of your efforts will be rewarded with great blessings.

In addition to its spiritual meaning, angel number 7777 represents prosperity, luck, good fortune, success in business endeavours, financial stability, health improvements, and positive relationships. It encourages us to stay positive even when faced with difficult challenges or obstacles because they are only temporary roadblocks on our journey towards our goals.

The angel number 7777 signifies inner peace as well as outer abundance in all aspects of life. It encourages us to maintain balance between our physical needs such as food and shelter while also nurturing our mental wellbeing through meditation or other forms of self-care activities. This angelic sign reminds us that we have the power within ourselves to create the life we desire if we stay focused on our goals while being mindful of our thoughts and intentions at all times.

Overall angel number 7777 is an empowering reminder from the divine realm that we are supported by the universe in all aspects of life and that we can manifest our dreams into reality if we stay focused on what truly matters most to us.

8888

The angel number 8888 is an incredibly powerful sign from the angels that the Universe is sending you a message of abundance, success, and prosperity. This number is a reminder to stay optimistic and maintain a positive attitude in all areas of your life. It can also signify that you are about to embark on a new journey in life – one that is filled with opportunities for growth and success.

The angel number 8888 is composed of four 8s, which symbolizes the infinite abundance available to us in the Universe. It's a reminder that we can have anything we desire if we just put our minds to it and take action. The 8's are also associated with karmic energy, which means that whatever we do or think will come back to us in kind. Therefore, it's important to stay focused on positive thoughts and actions if we want to attract more abundance into our lives.

When you see the angel number 8888, it's an indication that you have great potential for success and prosperity in your life right now. It's a reminder to trust your intuition and follow your heart when making decisions about how you want to live your life. This number encourages you to remain open-minded and take risks when necessary as this will help you reach your goals faster than if you were too afraid or hesitant to take action.

Overall, the angel number 8888 is a powerful sign from the angels that encourages us to stay optimistic, trust our intuition, and take action towards our goals so that we can achieve true abundance in all areas of our lives.

9999

The angel number 9999 is a powerful and meaningful message from the divine realm. It is a reminder that you have reached a point in your life where you can manifest your highest potential. The number 9999 resonates with the energies of completion, closure, and new beginnings.

When you see this number, it is an indication that you are ready to make a major shift in your life. It is a sign that it is time to let go of all that no longer serves you and to embrace your true purpose and potential. This angel number encourages you to take action towards achieving your goals and manifesting your dreams into reality.

The number 9999 also symbolizes service to humanity as well as spiritual enlightenment. It encourages you to be of service to others and use your gifts and talents for the greater good. This angel number brings with it an abundance of love, light, joy, and peace into your life.

Furthermore, the angel number 9999 signifies that the Universe is supporting you in all areas of your life. It encourages you to have faith in yourself and trust in the process of life even when things seem uncertain or difficult. This angel number reminds you that no matter what challenges come up along the way, everything will work out for the best if you stay focused on what truly matters most to you.

In conclusion, angel number 9999 is a reminder from the divine realm that it is time for transformation in all aspects of your life. It encourages us to take action towards achieving our goals and living our highest potentials while also being of service to others. The energies associated with this powerful angel number bring us strength, courage, faith, love, joy, abundance, and peace on our journey through life.